Cowboys, Jelly and Custard

Spirals Titles

Stories

Jim Alderson
Crash in the Jungle
The Witch Princess

Jan Carew
Death Comes to the Circus
Footprints in the Sand
Catchpole
Laura Called

Susan Duberley
The Ring

**Keith Fletcher and
Susan Duberley**
Nightmare lake

John Goodwin
Ghost Train
Dead-end Job

Paul Groves
Not that I'm Work-shy

Anita Jackson
The Actor
The Austin Seven
Bennet Manor
Dreams
The Ear
A Game of Life or Death
No Rent to Pay

Paul Jennings
Eye of Evil
Maggot

Margaret Loxton
The Dark Shadow

Patrick Nobes
Ghost Writer

David Orme
The Haunted Asteroids
City of the Roborgs

Kevin Philbin
Summer of the Werewolf

John Townsend
Beware the Morris Minor
Fame and Fortune
SOS
Night Beast

Plays

Jan Carew
Computer Killer
No Entry
Time Loop

John Godfrey
When I Count to Three

Paul Groves
Tell Me Where it Hurts

Barbara Mitchelhill
Punchlines
The Ramsbottoms at Home

Julie Taylor
Spiders

John Townsend
Cheer and Groan
Hanging by a Fred
The Lighthouse Keeper's Secret
Making a Splash
Over and Out
Taking the Plunge
Breaking the Ice
Cowboys, Jelly and Custard
Spilling the Beans
Rocking the Boat
A Minute to Kill
A Bit of a Shambles

David Walke
The Good, the Bad and the Bungle
Package Holiday

Cowboys, Jelly and Custard

John Townsend

Stanley Thornes (Publishers) Ltd

First published in 1994 by:
Stanley Thornes (Publishers) Ltd
Ellenborough House
Wellington Street
CHELTENHAM GL50 1YW
England

97 98 99 00 / 10 9 8 7 6 5 4

A catalogue record for this book is available from the British Library.

ISBN 0 7487 1879 6

Typeset by Tech-Set, Gateshead
Printed and bound in Great Britain at Martin's The Printers, Berwick

Contents

Knees Gone to Jelly

5 parts:
Buster Bludvessel, Clink, Poppy Jo, Flossy Sue, Big Bad Bob
(BBB)

Scene   *A smoky saloon in the very Wild West. It is night.*

Buster   This town is kind of quiet, ain't it, bartender?

Clink   Yip.

Buster   Too quiet.

Clink   Yip.

Buster   And this saloon is kind of . . . empty.

Clink   Yip.

Buster   And still.

Clink   Yip

Buster   Like a corpse.

Clink   Yip.

Buster   Kind of . . . spooky.

Clink	Yip.
Buster	Kind of . . . odd.
Clink	Yip.
Buster	Kind of . . . kind of . . . kind of. . . .
Clink	Scary?
Buster	Yip.
Clink	Yip.

[*Pause*]

Buster	So dead. I wonder why.
Clink	We're shut.
Buster	But it's gone sundown. Saloons always open at sundown.
Clink	Yip.
Buster	But no one's here.
Clink	Nope.
Buster	No sheriff.
Clink	Nope.
Buster	No cowboys.

Clink	Nope.
Buster	No nothing.
Clink	Nope.
Buster	Have you run out of beer, bartender?
Clink	Nope.
Buster	Then where are they all?
Clink	Trouble.
Buster	Trouble?
Clink	It's brewing.
Buster	Then you'd better send me a beer. Get a drink, Clink. What d'ya think?
Clink	Listen, mister, you're new around here but there's something you need to know.
Buster	Yip? What is it?

[*Enter Poppy Jo*]

Clink	You need to know . . . [*Whispering*] I can't tell you now, my daughter's come in.
Poppy Jo	How di do there, Pa. Why hello, mister.
Buster	Why howdy there, Miss Poppy Jo. You sure do look

9

	kind of pretty tonight.
Poppy Jo	Why thank you kind sir. I guess you're kind of cute too.
Clink	Here comes your beer, Buster.
Buster	Cheers! This will slip down real cool. [*Clink slides it down the bar to him*] Darn it! [*He misses*] It's gone all over me.

[*Enter Flossy Sue, swinging her hips and fluttering her eyelashes*]

Flossy Sue	Like you said, cowboy, it's slipped down real cool. And they don't come no cooler than you, Buster.
Clink	What are you doing out here tonight, Flossy Sue? Ain't you heard?
Flossy Sue	Sure, I've heard. I like action.
P.J.	What have you heard, Flossy Sue?
Clink	Go to your room, Poppy Jo. This is no place for a pure young girl.
Flossy Sue	What about me? Ain't I pure and young too?
Clink	You're only one of them words, Flossy Sue. Now all of you, you'd better get out of here. It's time.
Buster	But why? What's going on?

Clink	I told you. There's trouble.
Buster	What kind of trouble?
Clink	Bad trouble.
F.S.	Real trouble?
Clink	Double trouble.
F.S.	Treble trouble?
Clink	Double treble trouble.
Buster	That sure sounds like a lot of trouble!
Clink	The enemy. It won't be long now. It's evil.
Buster	Not . . . not . . . oh no, not Red Indians?
Clink	Worse than that.
Buster	There's nothing worse than that. I should know. Red Indians attacked our home when I was four. Red Indians dragged away my brother, Robby and killed him. Red Indians branded me with this mark on my hand. It's the sign of a wigwam burned with a red hot iron. Oh no, there's nothing worse than Red Indians.
P.J.	Oh no, I can think of nothing worse than a red hot iron on the back of your hand.

Buster	I can. I've got one somewhere else. I couldn't sit down for a month.
P.J.	Oh Buster, you poor boy. I want to cry.
Buster	So did I when they did it! But it's my Ma and Pa that never got over it. Every day they weep for my brother Robby. Poor little brother Robby.
P.J.	Don't say no more or I shall have to hug you like I've never hugged a man before.
Buster	The last I saw of my poor brother was his sad little face as he was dragged away on the back of a black stallion.
P.J.	No, stop or I'll fall into your arms in floods of tears and smother you in kisses.
Buster	I guess I'll just have to take the risk. I was the lucky one. You see, I was saved by this. [*He holds up a badge*]
Clink	A sheriff badge? A toy sheriff badge?
F.S.	You don't say that scared the Red Indians?
P.J.	It's got a big dent in it.
Buster	And do you know why? That badge stopped a bullet ripping through my heart. That badge saved

12

	my life. It's got the print of the bullet in the middle.
Clink	Let's take a look at that. Phewee, mister!
P.J.	Oh Buster. Oh Buster. Oh Buster! [*She hugs him*]
Buster	My heart has never been the same since.
P.J.	Why? Oh tell me why.
Buster	Because that badge was my little brother's badge. Yip, it was dear Robby's badge.
P.J	So you mean . . .
Buster	Yip. Robby should have been wearing the badge on that day. It should have been me who got carried away and he would have lived. Every day my heart weeps for little Robby. Every day I sob for that brother I lost.
P.J.	That's the saddest thing I ever did hear. [*Sob*]
Clink	You're a mighty fine boy.
F.S.	It's men like you who have made this country what it is today. [*Sniff*]
Buster	I guess so. Get us a drink, Clink. What d'ya think?
Clink	Have a beer on me, son. You're a mighty fine boy.

13

P.J.	Buster, what a sad story. I just want to hug you to death.
Buster	That's fine by me. I guess there are worse ways of dying! Go right ahead.
F.S.	I sure do like men who pull at my heart-strings.
Clink	Flossy Sue, you only like men when you pull at their purse-strings!

[*Sound of a loud gun shot from outside*]

P.J.	Eek! A shot!
Buster	Gee whiz!
Clink	A shot like that can only mean one thing.
P.J.	Oh no, Pa, not . . .
Clink	Yes. A gun has gone off.
Buster	Unless . . .
P.J.	Yes? What?
Buster	It could be a horse backfiring.
F.S.	So it must be true.
Buster	What's true, Flossy Sue?
F.S.	The news.

Buster	What news?
F.S.	The bad news.
P.J.	What bad news?
Clink.	Poppy Jo, go to your room and lock your door. [*He hides bottles and glasses*]
P.J.	But why, Pa? What is it?
F.S.	It's him.
Buster	Who?
F.S.	He's come back.
Clink	And he's out there.
P.J.	Who is it? Tell us.
F.S.	Shall I, Clink? What d'ya think, Clink?
Clink	I dunno.
F.S.	They'll have to know sometime.
Clink	Yes, but . . .
F.S.	He's back in town.
Buster	Who's back in town?
Clink	B.

F.S.	B.
Clink	B.
Buster	B?
P.J.	B?
F.S.	BBB.
Buster	BBB?
Clink	BBB.
P.J.	Who's BBB?
F.S.	Big Bad Bob.
Buster	Big Bad Bob? Who's that?

[*Saloon doors swing open. Enter Bob*]

Bob	Me! Bob. I'm big and bad and I'm back! With a great big 'B'.
Buster	Then how do you do? I'm Buster with a middle-sized 'B'.
Bob	I'm back to kill, with a great big 'K'. With muscles the size of a buffalo's.
Buster	A buffalo's what?
Clink	Go to your room, Poppy Jo.

P.J.	Sure, Pa.
Bob	You stay there. Say, that's kind of a pretty name, ain't it? Come here and let me touch you. I like the sweet smell of a pretty girl's hair.
Clink	Oh no!
P.J.	Surely not!
F.S.	Here we go, folks!
Bob	I'm waiting. I told you to come here, Poppy Jo. Come to BBB. Make it snappy.
Buster	Poppy Jo is quite happy where she is, thank you.
Bob	WHAT?
F.S.	Gasp!
P.J.	Gulp!
Bob	You weedy little wimp. Do you know who I am?
Buster	I think you've just told us. BBB ain't it?
Bob	Correct, with a great big 'K'. I'm Bob, d'ya hear? I've told ya what those other two 'B's stand for.
Buster	I've got a jolly good idea.
Bob	Good.

Buster	From where I'm standing, it's Bad Breath!
Bob	WHAT?
F.S.	Please don't!
P.J.	Jeepers!
Bob	Listen, kid. I don't know who you are or where you're from, but I don't like you. And that spells 'Git out o'here' with a great big 'GIT'. This town just ain't big enough for both of us.
Buster	Then you'd better go.
Clink	You've done it now, Buster. This guy is as mean as a skunk, as tough as an ox and as wild as a polecat.
Buster	True. He sings like a polecat, he thinks like an ox and he sure do pong like a skunk.
Bob	You don't have long to live, so make the most of it. If I get angry with a great big 'A', then this town dies with a great big 'D'. As it is, I'm going to rip your head off, chew off both ears and bite off those weedy little arms.
Buster	Are you sure you wouldn't prefer a Big Mac, extra fries, side-salad, green pepper and blue cheese?

Bob	I'm getting mad now with a great big 'M'. All day I've been riding across the plains. I've had the sun in my eyes. I've had the dust up my nose. All day I've had to fight the wind.
Buster	Serves you right for eating too many beans.
F.S.	He's done it now.
P.J.	Don't say no more, Buster.
Clink	Keep your heads down.
Bob	Come here and die! I'm gonna clean up this town. I'll get rid of scum like you. I'll be like a breath of fresh air in this place.
Buster	True. You're getting up my nose already.
Clink	Gulp!
P.J.	Darn it!
Bob	Don't it scare you to think of your throat being chewed up in a few seconds?
Buster	I guess a man's gotta chew what a man's gotta chew.
P.J.	Oh Buster, you're the bravest man I know.
F.S.	He's the daftest man I know.

Clink	He'll be the deadest man we know.
Bob	Get ready for pain with a great big 'P'. That's cruel with a great big 'K'. It'll hurt with a great big 'OUCH'.
P.J.	Please don't do it, BBB. Spare him, I beg you. I think I love him.
F.S.	Give him just one more chance.
Clink	Please don't snuff out a young life. Not in here, anyway - I've just had the walls cleaned.
Bob	No one gets in the way of BBB. I'm getting all het up.
F.S.	Then let me calm you down, BBB. I like a man who's big and strong and . . .
Buster	Ugly.
Bob	[*Thumping table and growling like a bear*] That's it with a great big 'I'. I will jump on you with a great big 'JUM'. I will thump you with a great big 'THUM'. I will bump you off with a great big 'BUM'.
Buster	And you sure do have a great big b . . . !
P.J.	Oh, Buster, you're such a wonderful man. How can you be so brave?

20

Buster	This bully can't scare me. It's because of my lucky charm. As long as I have that on, then no harm can come to me. That badge has saved my life hundreds of times. It protects me from vermin like him.
F.S.	Er . . . Buster, I feel you ought to know . . .
Buster	What's that, Flossy Sue?
F.S.	I dropped your badge into the trash can. You ain't got it on.
Buster	Hell, that's the worst news I've heard all day. It's what I call kind of scary. Now get it back quick or I'm a goner with a great big 'G'.
Clink	I can't seem to find it.
P.J.	Oh no!
Bob	Oh yeah!
Buster	Oh heck! My legs are giving way. My knees are jelly!
Bob	So now I've got ya! [*Steps forward with a roar*]
Buster	Gulp!
Bob	Now . . .
Buster	Yes?

Bob	I . . . [*Prodding Buster with each word*]
Buster	Eh?
Bob	Am . . .
Buster	What?
Bob	Going . . .
Buster	Where?
Bob	To . . .
Buster	Ah!
Bob	Rip . . .
Buster	Oh!
Bob	You . . .
Buster	Gosh!
Bob	Up . . .
Buster	Gulp!
Bob	Bit . . .
Buster	Gasp!
Bob	By . . .
Buster	Gee!

Bob	Bit . . .
Buster	Help!
Bob	[*Diving and grabbing him*] This will soon get r . . . [*He freezes while holding on to Buster*]
Buster	Er . . . is something the matter?
Bob	Mmmmmmmmm
P.J.	He seems to be frozen stiff.
F.S.	It's real odd.
Clink	His eyes have glazed over.
Buster	Like a trance.
P.J.	Like something just snapped.
Bob	No, not a trance. It's your hand.
Buster	I didn't touch you. Really, I didn't lay a finger on your body.
Bob	[*Letting him go*] That mark on your hand - a wigwam.
Buster	Burned by the Red Indians when I was four years old.
F.S.	He's also got one on his b . . .

Bob	You mean . . . like this? [*He lifts a sleeve to show one just the same*]
Clink	Flipperty jibbit!
F.S.	The man's gotta tattoo like this man's gotta tattoo!
Bob	The Red Indians burned it onto my arm when I was dragged away from home on a black stallion when I was a small boy.
P.J.	Why, Buster, you have a little silver tear running down your pale cheek.
Buster	And do you know why, Poppy Jo? I am moved. I think I am beginning to see a happy ending coming on.
F.S.	And BBB has little pearls of water filling those ice-blue eyes of his.
P.J.	The very same colour eyes as Buster's! And just look at their noses.
F.S.	The very same shape, and both need wiping! Are you thinking what I'm thinking?
P.J.	Noses must run in their family! The two grown men are sobbing!
Clink	Got it! I've found his special badge in the trash can. Look!

Bob	Show me that badge.
Buster	That was my brother's badge. My brother Robby, who was dragged away from home by Red Indians.
Bob	My brother's name was Buster. Is your name Buster Bludvessel?
Buster	Sure is.
Bob	I know because that was my badge. I was that brother. Buster, I am your long-lost brother Robby! [*They hug*]
Buster	You are alive!
Clink	Well I'll be blowed! [*They all weep*]
Bob	I have sinned. Will you forgive me? I have just felt love for the first time with a great big 'L'. I feel all warm inside.
Buster	Brother, I will love you till I die. [*They sob again*]
P.J.	Isn't this just so wonderful?
F.S.	So moving.
Clink	Kleenex coming up. [*He slides a box of tissues down the bar*]

Bob	I was held by the Red Indians for many years but one day I got away and I've been searching for something ever since.
P.J.	But why have you been so cruel and bad?
Bob	I guess I was just so chewed up inside. I was bitter and twisted. But now I will change. A man's gotta undo what a man's gotta undo.
Buster	You must come home. You will heal Ma's weak heart.
P.J.	Oh, Buster, let me come with you. You are the most wonderful man I have ever met.
Buster	Then let me here and now ask your father for your hand.
Clink	What do you want it for?
Buster	Clink, will you let me marry Poppy Jo? Get us a drink, Clink. What d'ya think?
Clink	Sure thing, Buster. Go right ahead. She's all yours.
Bob	And Flossy Sue, will you be my girl and ride away into the sunset with me? Will you be the woman to start my new life with me? Will you do that for me?

F.S.	You try and stop me, BBB. I just adore muscles like yours.
Bob	It's not BBB now. It's BBBB.
F.S.	BBBB?
Bob	Yip. Beautiful Brother Bobby Bludvessel.
P.J.	This is the happiest day of my life.
Buster	Then let's go. It's sunrise already.
Clink	Go and take one of my chickens to cook on the journey.
Buster	Thanks, Pa. A man's gotta cock-a-doodle-do what a man's gotta cock-a-doodle-do! [*Buster and Poppy Jo exit*]
Bob	And you come with me, Flossy Sue. Goodbye, Clink. Goodbye, saloon. Goodbye, town. A man's gotta toodle-oo when a man's gotta toodle-oo! [*They exit*]
Clink	Well that's it, then! Gone. So that's the tale of two brothers, the Bludvessels and Poppy, the heroine. But just remember, folks, what heroine does to blood vessels! It usually all ends in vain and everything goes to pot! So beware and just remember, folks, don't you try this play at home. Cheers y'all!

Lumps in the Custard

5 parts:
Miss Rhubarb Clingfilm (Ruby), Mrs Ivy Clingfilm (Ma),
Grandpa (Pop), Billy Hillbill, Ashley Frimple

*Scene   The parlour of the Clingfilm home in the deep deep
South.* Grandpa *is asleep in the corner.* Rhubarb *rushes in,
excited.*

Ruby	Only another half hour! Oh how my heart beats faster. Oh how my breath gasps in short pants.
Pop	Short pants? Where?
Ruby	Oh, Grandpa, I didn't see you there. I am so thrilled. I am over the moon. Isn't love wonderful?
Pop	Blowed if I can remember.
Ruby	I've seen the man of my dreams. Ashley Frimple. He'll be here in this very room in twenty-nine minutes, to meet Ma.
Pop	Will that be wise, Ruby, honey child?
Ruby	Well, he has to meet her soon because she still knows nothing of him.

Pop	And that's the best thing!
Ruby	But don't you see, Grandpa? We're getting wed.
Pop	Wed?
Ruby	Oh yes. We've fallen in love, head over heels.
Pop	Jeepers! How did you meet a man without your Ma getting to hear?
Ruby	Oh we haven't met yet. But we will soon. Just twenty eight minutes!
Pop	But if you ain't met yet, then how the cotton-pickin' jeepers do you know he wants to wed you?
Ruby	He sent me a note which I keep by my heart. He's so handsome.
Pop	How can you tell? Your Ma never lets you look at a man.
Ruby	We're just made for each other. His smile says it all, I just know it. Why, right now he will be getting ready to come and take my hand. He'll be slipping into his best suit. Oh, how wicked of me even to think of him undressed! What would Ma say?
Pop	She'd say far too much as always. And far too loud.

Ruby	Oh Grandpa, you understand me, don't you?
Pop	Course I do. I was young once. I'm jiggered if I can remember it though. We all have our secrets from your Ma – like my secret bottle I hide under the stairs. Like my box of baccy I keep under the bed. Like my secret with Billy Hillbill.
Ruby	Billy Hillbill?
Pop	The horse man. He's coming round to see me soon to give me a few tips for a horse I'm thinking of betting on. Little Darling, that's her name.
Ruby	But Grandpa, gambling is a sin!
Pop	Then whatever you do, don't tell your Ma.
Ruby	Very well, Grandpa. Your sin is safe with me.
Pop	And yours is safe with me.
Ruby	But I haven't sinned, Grandpa.
Pop	That's not how your Ma will think of it. If you've so much as spoken about a man coming to this house, then you'll need to scrub your mouth out with three bars of soap.
Ruby	Yes. Ma does have strong views about men. But anyway, I am twenty-two!

Ma	[*Calling from outside*] Rhubarb! Rhubarb!
Ruby	I'm in the parlour, Ma. Oh dear, I hope she understands.
Pop	Well, if I were a betting man, which I wish I could be, I wouldn't bet on it! I'll make myself kind of scarce. My old heart can't stand her screams. [*He hobbles off*]

[*Enter Ma, looking fierce*]

Ma	Tuck that shirt in, Pop. You look like a heap of garbage. Now then, Rhubarb, it's time you had a lie down in your room. A lady needs a rest in the afternoons.
Ruby	But I'd like a word with you, Ma.
Ma	Make it quick. I have things to do.
Ruby	It's . . . it's . . . well, someone will be calling at our door soon.
Ma	And who might that be?
Ruby	Just . . . a man.
Ma	A what?
Ruby	A man.

Ma	Rhubarb, I have told you never to say that word. You know what I think about men, ever since your Pa ran off with the washer-woman. Men are all the same, just like your Pa. He was nothing but a dirty old man.
Ruby	Then the washer-woman was probably the best thing for him.
Ma	The neighbours still don't talk to me even after twenty years.
Ruby	That might be because you shot their cat, Ma.
Ma	It was a tomcat. I hate all males.
Ruby	But Grandpa is a good man. You love him, don't you?
Ma	Of course not. He's like all the rest of them. He just eats, sleeps and always gets in the way. The only good man is a dead one.
Ruby	Then why do you let him stay here?
Ma	Simple. Dollars. Where there's a will, there's a way. I only get the family pearl so long as he stays here and you stay single.
Ruby	But what about Ashley?
Ma	Who?

Ruby	Ashley Frimple. He's coming here soon.
Ma	Rhubarb!
Ruby	No, it's true.
Ma	Rubbish, I've told you before. Never let a man set eyes on you. Never think of such a wicked thing.
Ruby	But . . . but . . . I love him.
Ma	You what?
Ruby	I've fallen in love with Ashley Frimple. He's so tall and dark and . . .
Ma	Rhubarb Clingfilm! Just you get down on your knees and pray. Whatever has gotten into you, girl?
Ruby	But Ma, I've never even said hello to a man. I'm twenty-two.
Ma	And that was the age I married your Pa. Look what became of him. They're all the same. Now get to your room and have a cold bath.
Ruby	He'll be here any minute. He's come to ask you if I can be his wife. He wants my hand.
Ma	And he'll get mine - across his face. How dare you say such things?

Ruby	[*Sobbing*] Oh no, please. Allow me just to look into his eyes, to see his smile and to whisper into his ear.
Ma	Out! Get up in that bath tub to scrub your sins away.
Ruby	Sniff! Sob! [*She exits*]
Ma	I won't hear of it. If she marries, then I lose the family pearl. It says so in the deeds. No. Rhubarb stays here. [*Knock at the door*] So this must be the wretch. Ashley Frimple, you get ready to meet your match. I'll enjoy this. [*Opening door*] Yes?
Billy	Er, I've come about Little Darling.
Ma	Come in. [*Under her breath*] You toad! Now, let's get a few facts straight. Phew! There's a strong smell of horses in the air.
Billy	Well yes, that's because . . .
Ma	Be quiet. I know why you're here.
Billy	You know? I thought it was a secret. You know about the little filly?
Ma	How dare you! Where did you meet her?
Billy	In the stables.

Ma	What? When?
Billy	Every night. I keep my eye on her. You see I've got an eye for rare little beauties like her. She'll go a long way.
Ma	You evil toad. Have you ever . . . touched her?
Billy	Pardon me, ma'am?
Ma	I said, have you ever laid a finger on her?
Billy	Of course. She needs a rub-down every day. Only yesterday I sat on her back and gave her a sugar lump.
Ma	What?
Billy	You take my advice. She's the one to put your money on.
Ma	What the blazes are you saying?
Billy	I've never seen legs like it.
Ma	Stop! You evil swine.
Billy	And such a fine body, too. So strong and solid. Built to last.
Ma	Tell me straight, have you ever . . . kissed her?
Billy	Beg your pardon, ma'am?

Ma	Tell me, yes or no. Have you kissed her? Have you ever been out with her? Have you had dinner together with soft music, soft lights and wine?
Billy	Oh no. Just hay, the odd carrot and a bucket of bran.
Ma	Well, that's something. But how could she fall for a scruff like you?
Billy	But she's never fallen. Strong as an ox is that fine beast. Takes after her mother, the tough old nag. And she loves a good tickle on her neck and a slap on the behind to get her to gallop.
Ma	Get out! You've said enough! [*She throws him out and leaves the door open*]

[*Enter Pop*]

Pop	Er, did I happen to hear voices?
Ma	Some fool. Little darling, indeed! Now then, you're coming with me upstairs to have your hair trimmed.
Pop	But I . . .
Ma	No 'buts'. You'll do as you're told. [*She drags him off as a head pops round the door. Enter Ashley Frimple*]
Ashley	Cooee! Why hello? Anyone at home? I say, cooee!

[Enter Ruby, sobbing helplessly]

Ruby   Oh what can I do? Oh where can I go? Life is so cruel - to say nothing of Ma.

Ashley   Why, how do you do, Miss Rhubarb?

Ruby   Oh Ashley!

Ashley   Oh Rhubarb!

Ruby   Oh Ashley, you're here.

Ashley   Oh Ruby, you're here too.

Ruby   I live here, Ashley. Ashley, oh Ashley, say you love me, Ashley.

Ashley   You love me, Ashley. Let me hold you in my arms.

Ruby   What about Ma?

Ashley   I can't hold both of you!

Ruby   No, no. If she finds you here in the parlour, she will kill you.

Ashley   Then let's go in the kitchen.

Ruby   But she'll kill you there, too.

Ashley   From here?

Ruby   She could kill a man a mile away.

Ashley	Can she shoot?
Ruby	With her tongue. She says such cruel things. She can kill at forty paces. Oh, Ashley, are you going to sweep me off my feet? Are you going to carry me off in those powerful arms? Are you going to ride off into the sunset with me by your side forever?
Ashley	It looks that way, Rhubarb.
Ruby	Ruby. Please call me Ruby, Ashley.
Ashley	Anything you say, Ruby Ashley.
Ruby	Would you cross mountains for me, Ashley? Would you? Would you leap canyons for me, Ashley? Would you? Would you wade through swamps, snake pits and Red Indian country for me, Ashley? Would you? Well?
Ashley	You bet, Ruby.
Ruby	How wonderful! A man who's scared of nothing!
Ashley	You bet, Ruby.
Ruby	I'll go and get Ma.
Ashley	Ooer! [*He faints*]
Ruby	[*Rushing to him*] Ashley, Ashley, are you all right? Speak to me. This is the first time I have held a

man's face in my hands. The first time I have
stroked his cheek. The first time I will kiss him on
his forehead. I think I'll rather like it.

[*Enter Ma, as Ruby kisses him*]

Ma	Rhubarb! Put that man down!
Ruby	Must I?
Ma	Pop, come here! Go and get the gun and pump that man full of lead.
Pop	Does that mean he won't be staying for tea?
Ashley	[*Leaping up with a knife*] Oh no you don't! [*He holds it to Ruby's cheek*] Nobody move or she dies.
Pop	Anything you say.
Ruby	But Ashley, we were in love!
Ma	Now ain't that just like a man? The lousy good-for-nothing double-crossing toe-rag.
Ashley	I was only acting.
Ruby	Acting?
Pop	You call that acting?
Ashley	It's not Ruby I want. I really came here to get my hands on . . .

Ruby	What?
Ma	Yes?
Pop	You can't mean . . .
Ashley	Yes. Not the Clingfilm Ruby but the Clingfilm Pearl. I've come to steal it. Hand it over.
Ma	Never.
Ruby	But Ma, he'll kill me.
Ashley	That's right. I'll kill her if I don't get my way.
Ma	Then it's just one of those unlucky days.
Ashley	I've got no time for games. Hand it over, Grandpa. Go get it.
Pop	Sure. Anything you say.
Ma	Pop, you stay right there. That pearl stays where it is.
Ruby	Oh no, this is the worst day in the whole of my life. [*Sobs*]
Ashley	This could be the *last* day in the whole of your life. If I don't see that pearl by the time I count to three, this Rhubarb will be well and truly stewed. I hope I make myself clear.

Ma	Darn it. All that I've waited for will be gone with the wind.
Ruby	Ashley, Ashley, tell me you love me.
Ma	Rhubarb! Pull yourself together.
Ruby	Oh no, please no. No . . . no . . . NO!
Ma	You're starting to crumble, Rhubarb. Don't be a fool, Rhubarb.
Ashley	Here goes! One . . .
Ruby	Please!
Ashley	Two . . .
Ruby	Don't!
Pop	I think he means it.
Ma	Dash shame.
Ashley	Three . . . Aaah!

[*Enter Billy. He leaps in the air, kicks the knife free and socks Ashley on the jaw*]

Billy	Aah! Let go of that pure young maiden, you wretch. Now go, before I shoot you between the eyes and

	skin you like a rattlesnake, string you up like a buffalo or lasso you like a bison. Do you know what I do with a bison?
Ashley	Oh no. What do you do with a bison?
Billy	Wash my hands in it, of course.
Ashley	Now that's what I call bad. I can't stand jokes like that. [*Exits*]
Ruby	Who is this man?
Ma	Not that smelly old hillbilly again.
Billy	[*Removing his old hat and coat*] Not any more! It was all a cover-up! I am Captain Bill Custard, US Army, at your service. My men have got this place surrounded and will take him away.
Ma	Men?
Ruby	Custard?
Billy	Yes. Very smooth, tasty and just right with a little . . . Rhubarb!
Ma	Then take a seat by the fire, Captain Custard.
Billy	Well, I don't mind if I do, thank you kindly, ma'am. [*He sits*]

Pop	So that's Custard's last stand!
Ma	You seem cold, Custard.
Billy	Just a trifle.
Ruby	I think I love him.
Billy	Will you marry me?
Ruby	You bet!
Billy	Then that's that!
Pop	Well doggone! That was quick.
Billy	Oh yes, they don't call me Instant Custard for nothing!
Ruby	And I shall be called Rhubarb Custard.
Billy	We must have been made for each other! [*They hug*]
Ma	Rhubarb! Let go of that man. I won't have such evil things going on under my roof.
Ruby	Then we'd better go outside in the yard.
Pop	Just how did you know we were being held in here at knife point, soldier?

Billy	We've been watching your house for days. At last we've got that bandit. We're only sorry we had to use you as bait, Ruby. At least you'll get the handsome reward.
Ruby	But not as handsome as you, Captain! But how did you know about me?
Billy	For days I have been sitting in the tree outside your room, just gazing up into your window.
Ma	You're blushing, Rhubarb.
Pop	Yeah, you've gone right real rich ruby red, Ruby.
Ruby	But I take a bath in my room every day, right in front of my window.
Billy	That's right! Don't worry, miss. I kept this little eye real shut.
Ruby	But what about the other eye?
Billy	It was kept well and truly hidden . . .
Ruby	Good.
Billy	. . . by the end of the telescope. But now we've got our man.
Ruby	And so have I.

Billy	That man was wanted all over town.
Ruby	I'm not suprised. He was so handsome.
Billy	No. His face is on all the Wanted posters in town.
Pop	You don't say!
Billy	Yip. Mister Rocky Crags, the bandit. The toughest guy in town. And now we've got him, thanks to you, Miss Ruby. The reward money's yours!
Ruby	A tough guy is so good to find but a good guy is so tough to find. But I found one of each in one day! Do you think he really would have killed me just then?
Billy	Sure thing. You bet. He tied his last victim to the railroad track.
Ruby	The railroad track? But why?
Billy	To make her talk. But she didn't say a word.
Ruby	Well, how did she manage that?
Billy	The train came early.
Pop	She must have been a mighty proud woman.

Billy	Sure. She was chuffed to bits.
Ma	Now ain't that just like a man?
Billy	Mrs Clingfilm, will you let Miss Rhubarb be mine forever?
Ma	But what about that there pearl?
Billy	Keep it. We won't want that. We've got each other and the reward money.
Ma	Bah, don't it make ya sick?
Billy	Look, I've already got a diamond ring for Miss Ruby. And I've even got a diamond for you, Mrs Clingfilm, to keep with that pearl of yours. After all, you know what they say.
Pop	Nope. What's that, mister?
Billy	A diamond is a pearl's best friend. I feel a very proud man. I have a lump in my throat at the thought of us together.
Pop	You mean you feel all lumpy, Custard?
Ma	I guess I feel my heart beginning to warm. Pop, go and open that secret bottle of whisky of yours so we can drink a toast.

Pop	How did you know that I keep a bottle hidden under the third floorboard under the stairs?
Ma	I didn't – but I sure do now. You toad. I suppose you keep a secret box of baccy with it.
Pop	Oh no, that's under the bed. Oops! Darn it!
Ma	Oh no it ain't. I changed it years ago for minced rattlesnake.
Billy	So, Miss Ruby, will you be my bride? Can I take you by the hand and ask you to be mine? We'll fill our home with the patter of little Custards. Allow me to kiss your Ruby cheeks and your Ruby lips. Well, what is your answer?
Ruby	Well, after all, you know what they say.
Pop	Nope. What's that, Ruby?
Ruby	Yip! Yahoo!
Pop	Gee, now ain't that real cute? What a fine couple. And after all, you know what they say.
Ma	Nope. What's that, Grandpa?
Pop	It's time you two were getting the doggone, cotton-pickin', nut-crunchin', hum-dingin', yankee-

doodlin', rootin'-tootin', cool-doodin', chicken-lickin', gee-whizin', hill-billyin' candy-suckin' out of here!

Ma	You what, Pop?
Ruby	You what, Pop?
Billy	You what, Pop?
Pop	It's the corn-poppin' end. Yeehow!